THIS JOURNAL BELONGS TO:

_____

selah

PAUSE, LISTEN, PRAISE.

ALEXIS

Copyright © 2022 Alexis Delaney

All rights reserved. No part of this publication may be reproduced, distributed, or transmitted in any form or by any means, including photocopying, recording, or other electronic or mechanical methods, without the prior written permission of the publisher, except in the case of brief quotations embodied in critical reviews and certain other noncommercial uses permitted by copyright law. For permission requests, write to the publisher, addressed "Attention: Permissions Coordinator," at the address below.

Paperback: 978-1-951475-26-0
Library of Congress Control Number: 2022914113
First paperback edition: October 2022

Any references to historical events, real people, or real places are used fictitiously.

Names, characters, and places are products of the author's imagination.

Illustrated by Amanda Blake Design
Layout by Amanda Blake Design

Arrow Press Publishing
Charleston, SC
www.arrowpresspublishing.com

SECTION 1

Introduction

SECTION 2

Sermon Notes

SECTION 3

Prayer Hub

SECTION 4

Rhema

SECTION 5

Conclusion

And you will seek Me
and find Me, when

*you search for Me
with all your heart.*

JEREMIAH 29:13 NKJV

SECTION 1

one

introduction

USING THE WEEKLY PRAYER HUB SECTION

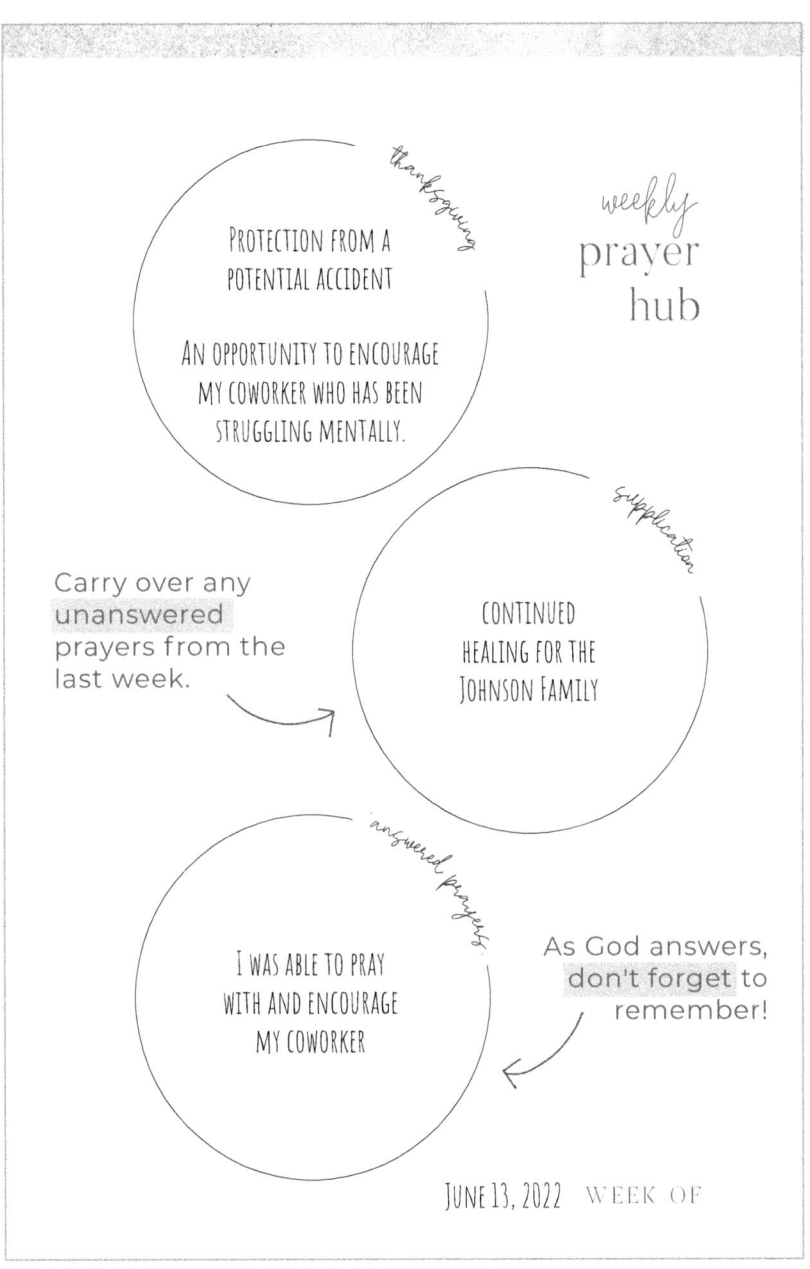

USING THE INTERCESSION CIRCLES

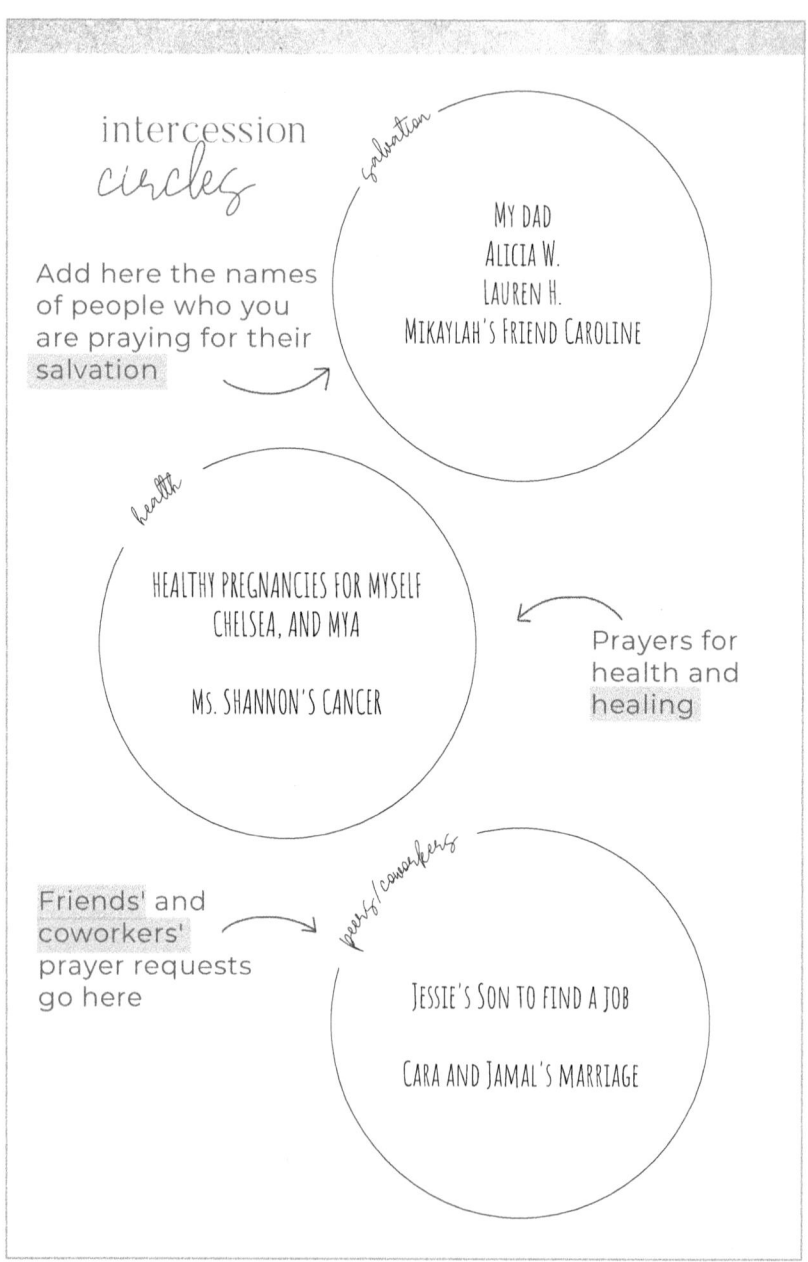

Intercession for **the leaders** in your life →

leaders

- Pastor Isaiah
- President and leaders of the US
- Principals at Arian's school

How can God move in your **relationships**? →

relationships

- Closer relationship with my sisters
- God would send me a spiritual mother
- Work relationships

Don't forget to write down the prayers God answered ↓

answered **prayers**

6/26/22 - My dad received salvation

7/07/22 - Jessie's son was offered a job

USING THE SERMON NOTES SECTION

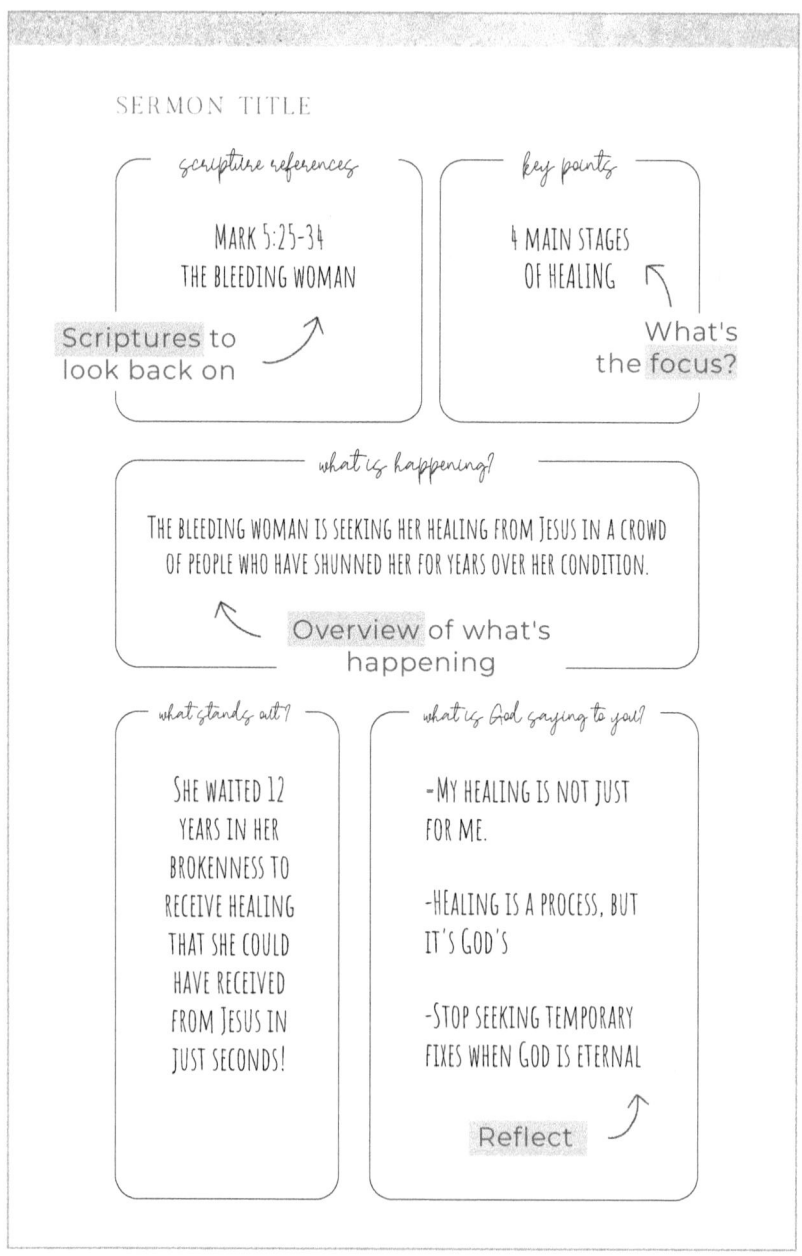

DATE 6/26/22

- The bleeding woman had been seeking healing from worldly resources - doctors, medicine, etc.

- She finally let go of what she could do and leaned on God

- Instead of staying in her condition, she went out of her comfort zone, into town, where she had been shunned and considered unclean.

- Even though she was uncomfortable she pushed through for healing.

- She touched Jesus garment and was physically healed.

- When Jesus acknowledged what had happened, the woman "told Him the whole truth" this was her Spiritual Healing!

- The last stage of her healing process is the remodeling stage - changing the narrative of her condition, from broken to redeemed.

- Seeing others healed and set free from the healing, she received from Jesus. her testimony! WOW!

Here take your notes on the message

USING THE RHEMA PAGES

DATE 6/30/22

6 pieces of armor

1. Belt of Truth - holds the armor together. All the pieces of armor are dependent on the belt of truth - vs. 14

2. Breastplate of Righteousness - holy character without moral character, you're left vulnerable - vs. 14

3. Gospel of Peace - allows us to advance in war with confidence The Lord is with us - vs. 15

4. Shield of Faith - Protects us from doubt, we can believe God's promises protection from lies - vs. 16

5. Helmet of Salvation - we can have hope in the fact that we will be with Jesus, the assurance of salvation allows us to be fearless in battle - vs. 17

6. Sword of the Spirit - the "rhema" word of God. This means specific relevant scripture pertaining to the specific battle. Holy Spirit guides us to attack the enemy with God's word strategically - vs. 17

PROMPTS

What vision of your calling has God given you, if any? If you're not sure what your calling is, write out a prayer asking God to show you or give you clarity in that area.

_____
_____
_____
_____
_____
_____

What is something you wish to accomplish in the next year?

_____
_____
_____

What is something you wish to accomplish in the next five years?

_____
_____
_____

Is there something God is asking you to do, whether it be to write a book, forgive someone, or spend more time with Him? Write it here

_____
_____
_____
_____
_____
_____
_____
_____
_____
_____
_____
_____
_____
_____
_____
_____
_____
_____
_____
_____
_____
_____
_____
_____
_____

But he who looks into the perfect law of liberty and continues in it, and is not a forgetful hearer but a doer of the word, *this one will be blessed in what he does.*

JAMES 1:25

SECTION 2

sermon notes

SERMON TITLE

scripture references

key points

what is happening?

what stands out?

what is God saying to you?

DATE

SERMON TITLE

scripture references

key points

what is happening?

what stands out?

what is God saying to you?

DATE

SERMON TITLE

scripture references

key points

what is happening?

what stands out?

what is God saying to you?

DATE

SERMON TITLE

scripture references

key points

what is happening?

what stands out?

what is God saying to you?

DATE

SERMON TITLE

scripture references

key points

what is happening?

what stands out?

what is God saying to you?

DATE

SERMON TITLE

scripture references

key points

what is happening?

what stands out?

what is God saying to you?

DATE

SERMON TITLE

scripture references

key points

what is happening?

what stands out?

what is God saying to you?

DATE

SERMON TITLE

scripture references

key points

what is happening?

what stands out?

what is God saying to you?

DATE

SERMON TITLE

scripture references

key points

what is happening?

what stands out?

what is God saying to you?

DATE

SERMON TITLE

scripture references

key points

what is happening?

what stands out?

what is God saying to you?

DATE

SERMON TITLE

scripture references

key points

what is happening?

what stands out?

what is God saying to you?

DATE

SERMON TITLE

scripture references

key points

what is happening?

what stands out?

what is God saying to you?

DATE

But seek first the kingdom of God and His righteousness, and all these things *shall be added to you.*

MATTHEW 6:33

SECTION 3

prayer hub

intercession
circles

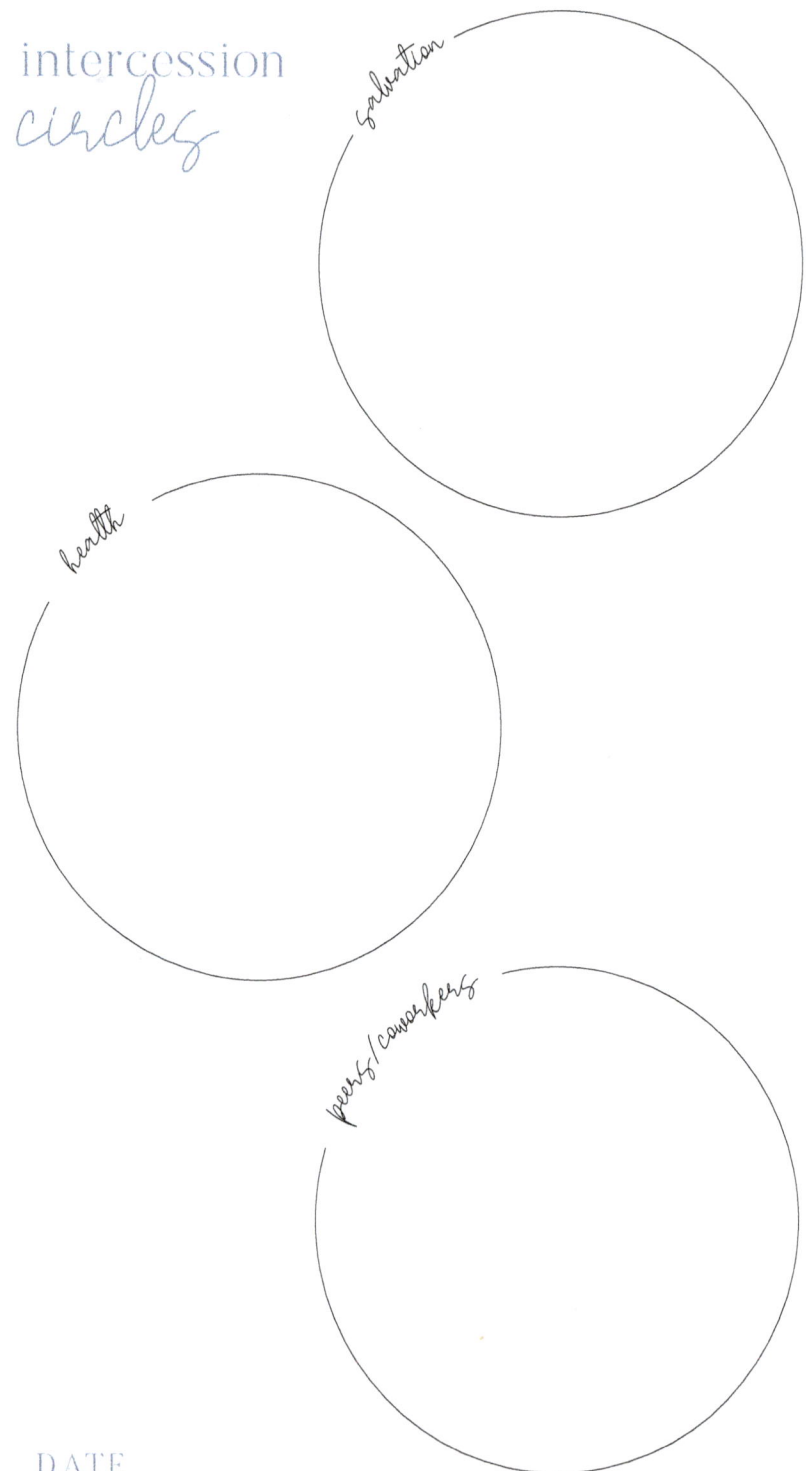

- salvation
- health
- peers/coworkers

DATE

leaders

relationships

answered
prayers

weekly prayer hub

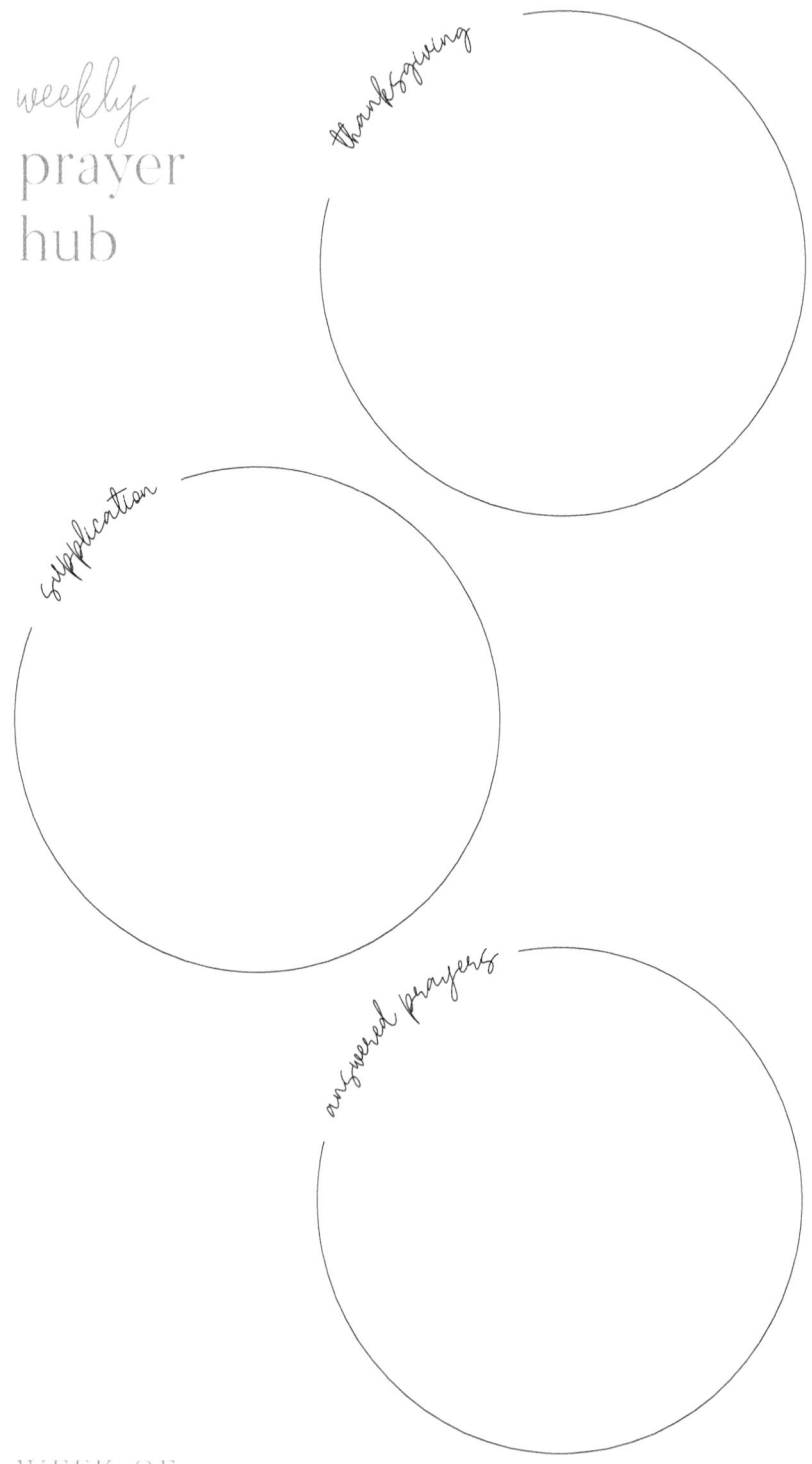

thanksgiving

supplication

answered prayers

WEEK OF

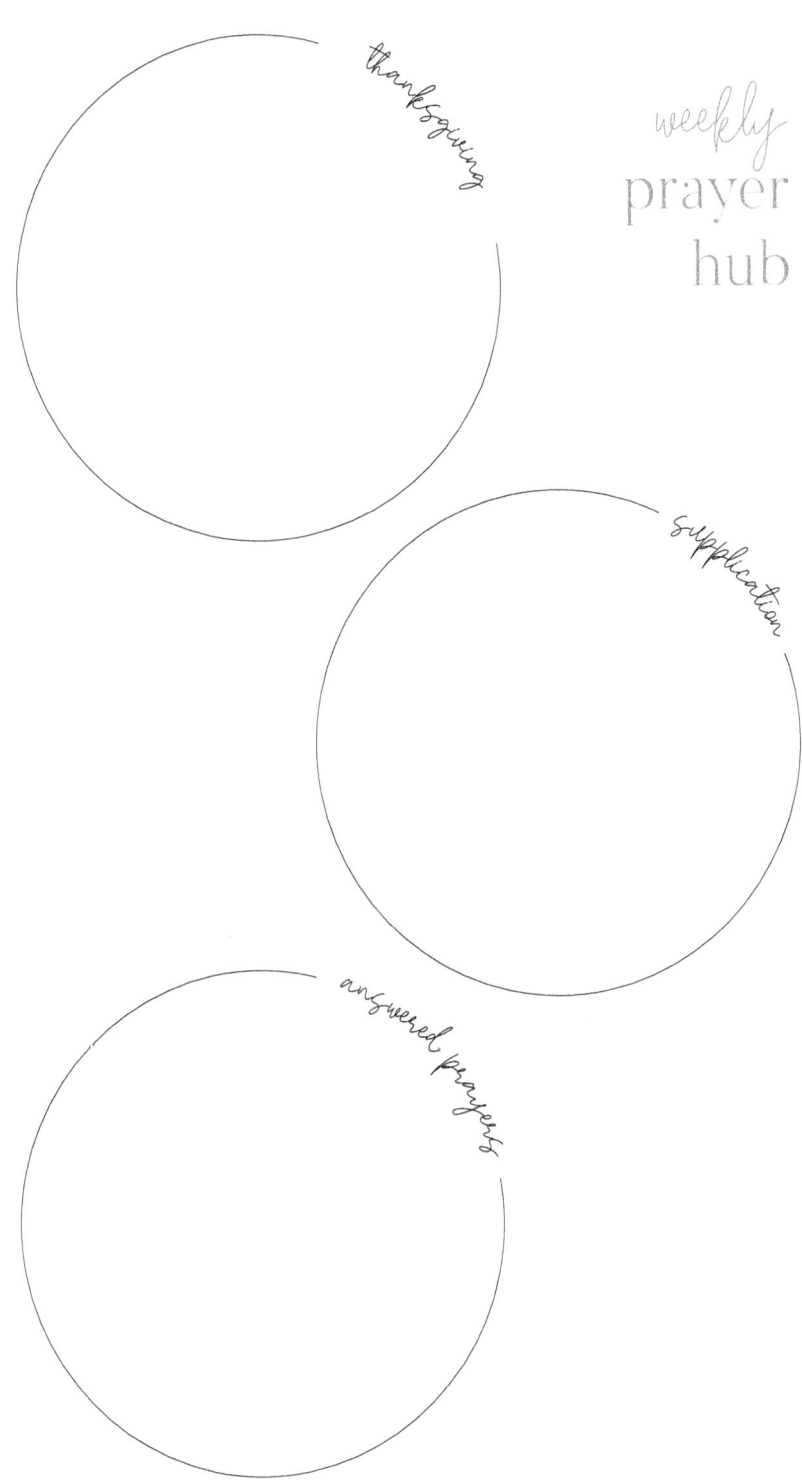

weekly
prayer
hub

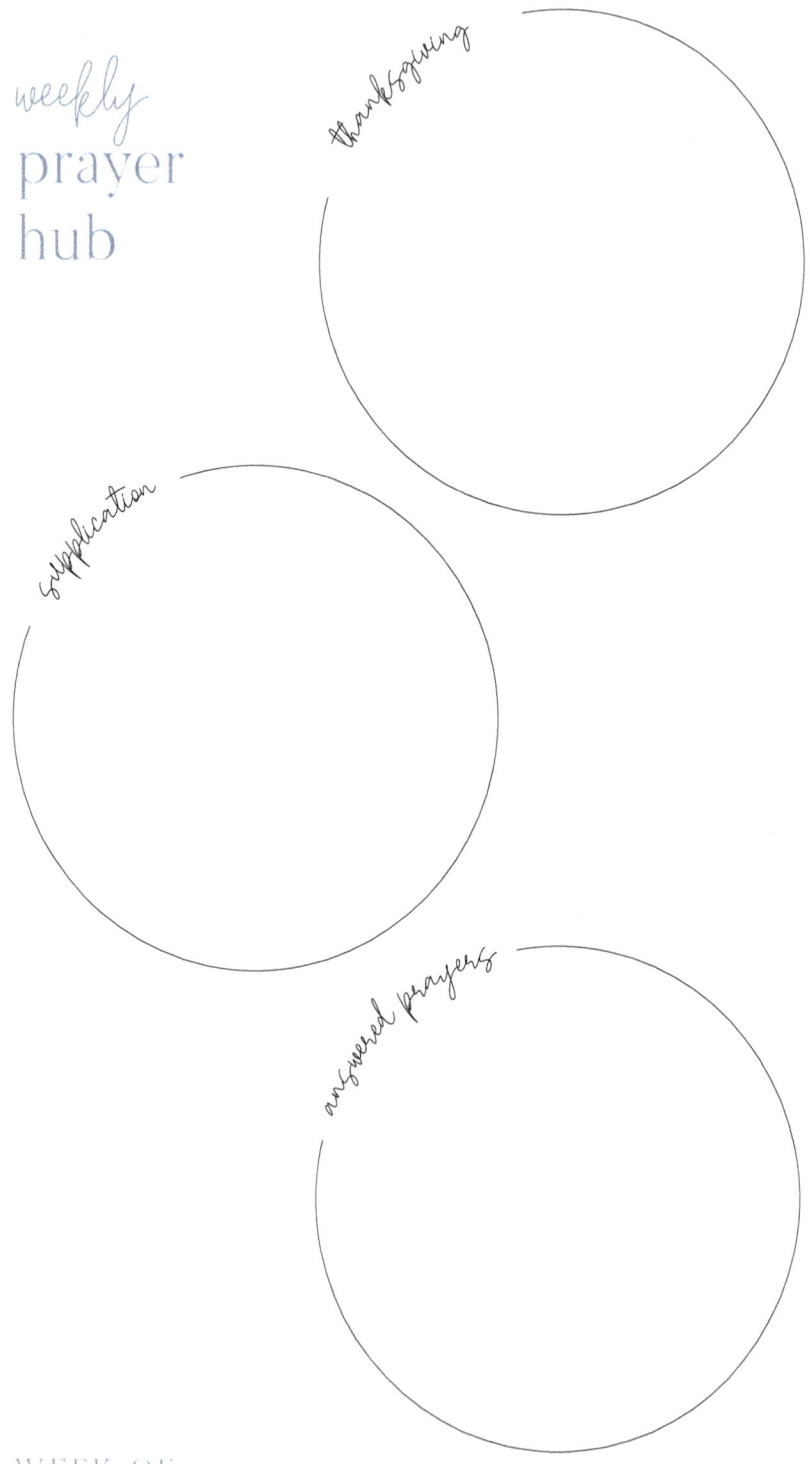

thanksgiving

supplication

answered prayers

WEEK OF

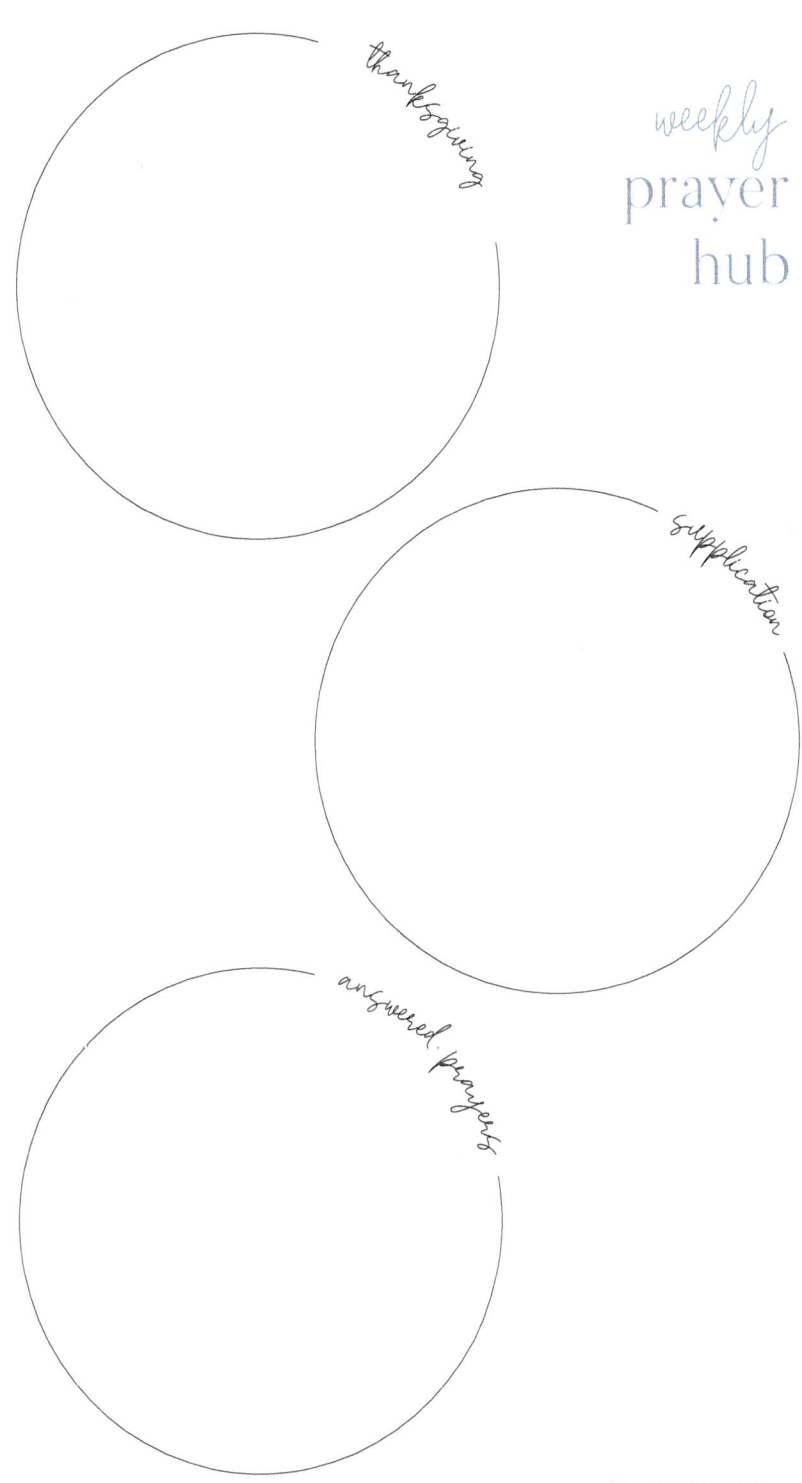

thanksgiving

weekly prayer hub

supplication

answered prayers

WEEK OF

weekly
prayer
hub

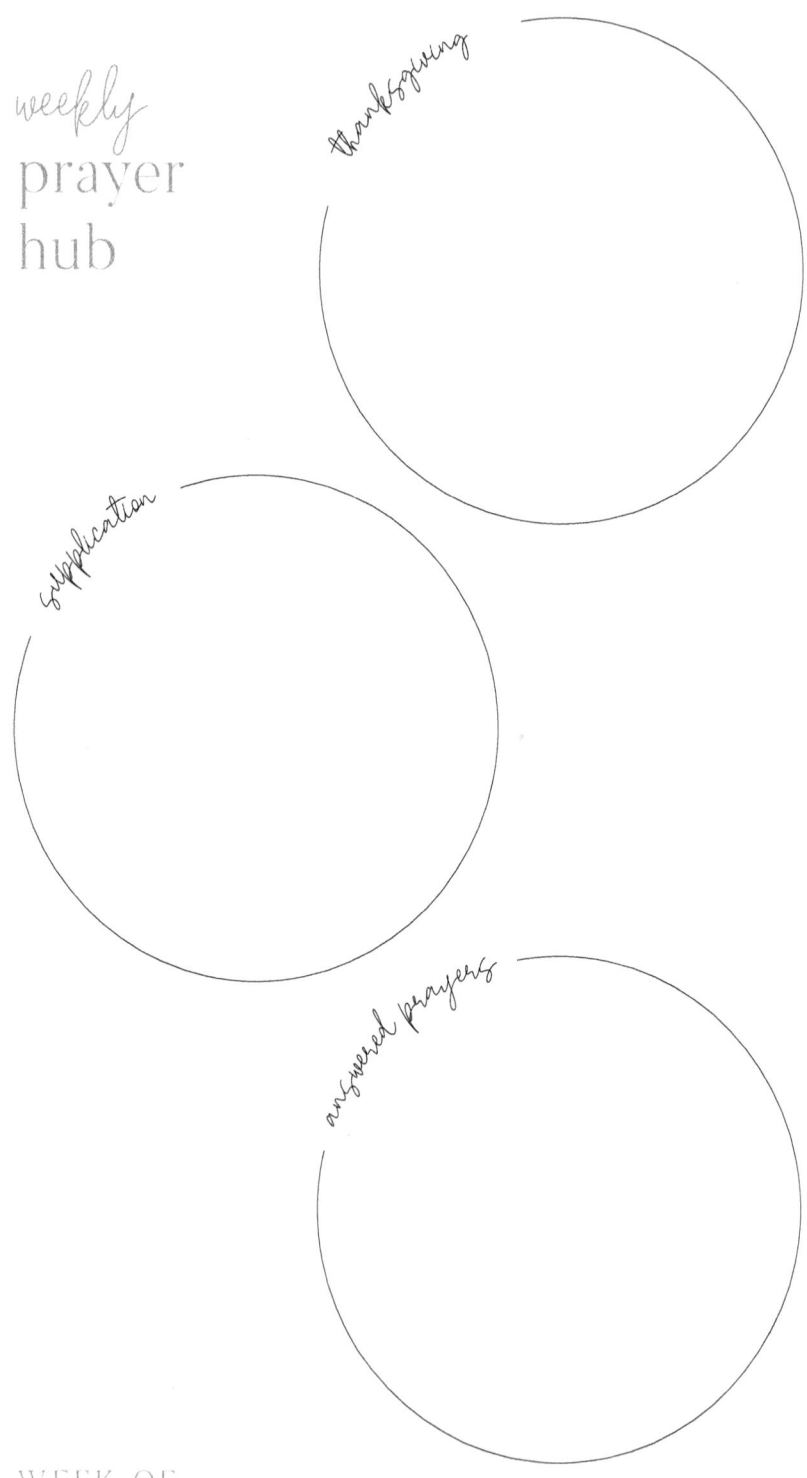

thanksgiving

supplication

answered prayers

WEEK OF

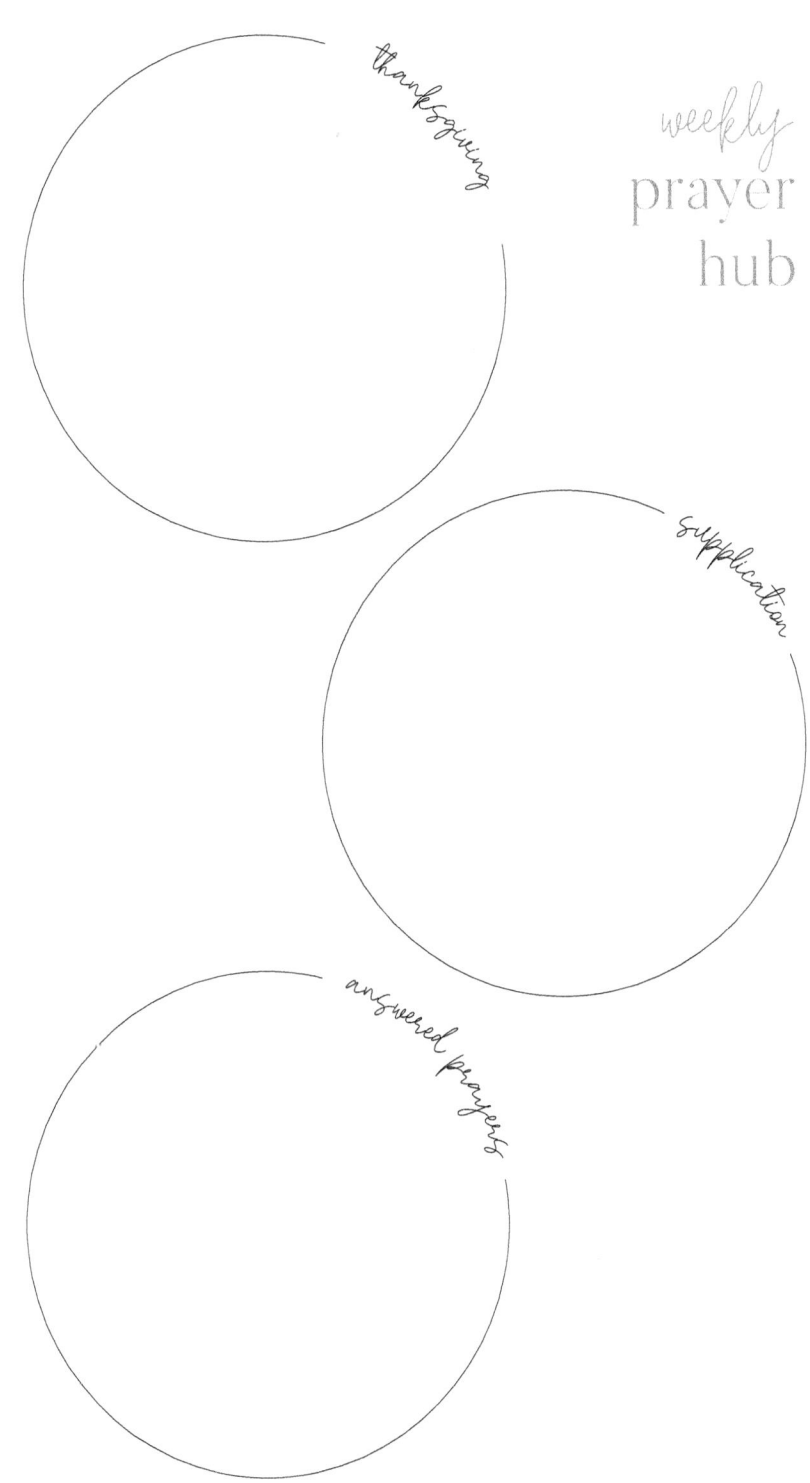

weekly prayer hub

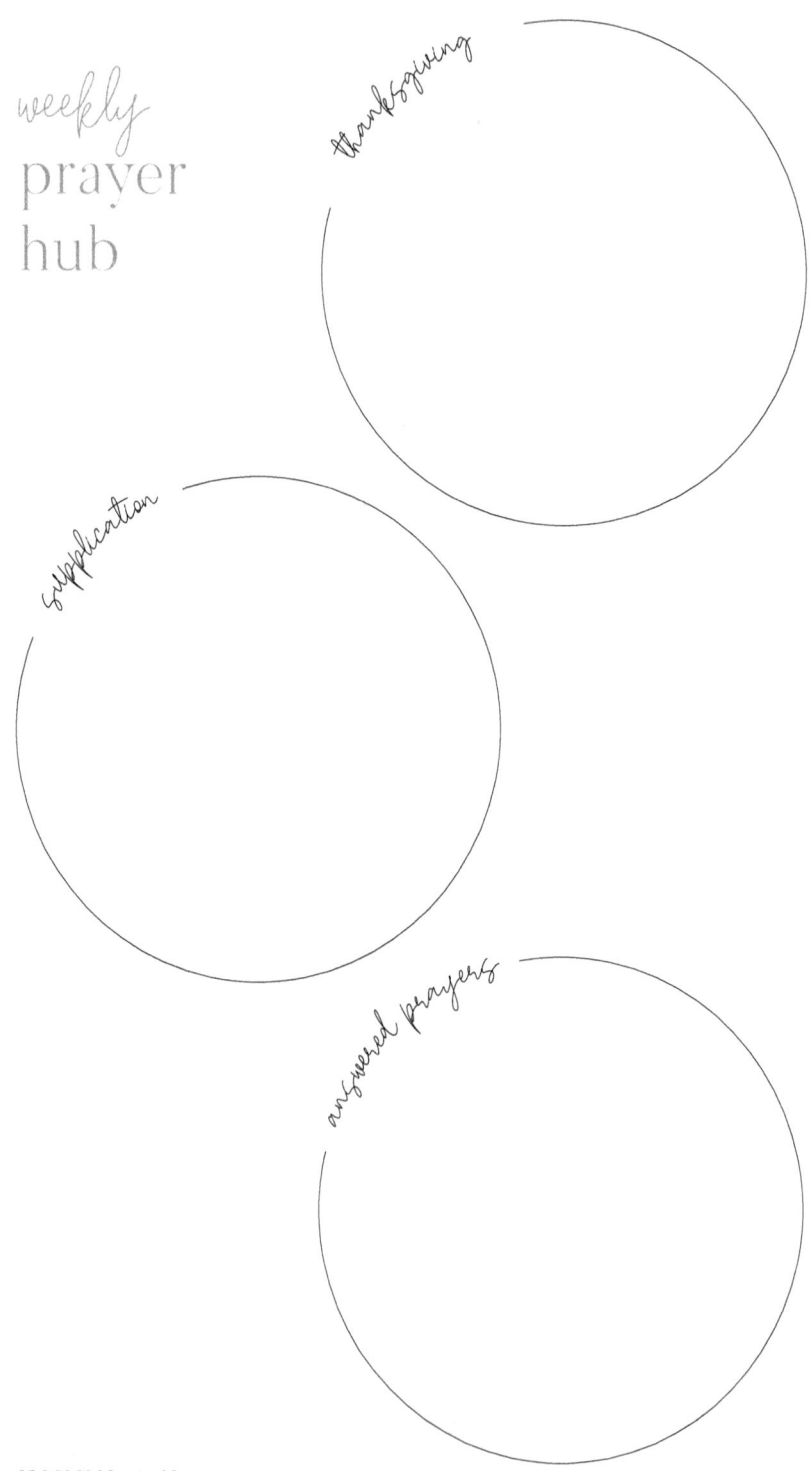

- thanksgiving
- supplication
- answered prayers

WEEK OF

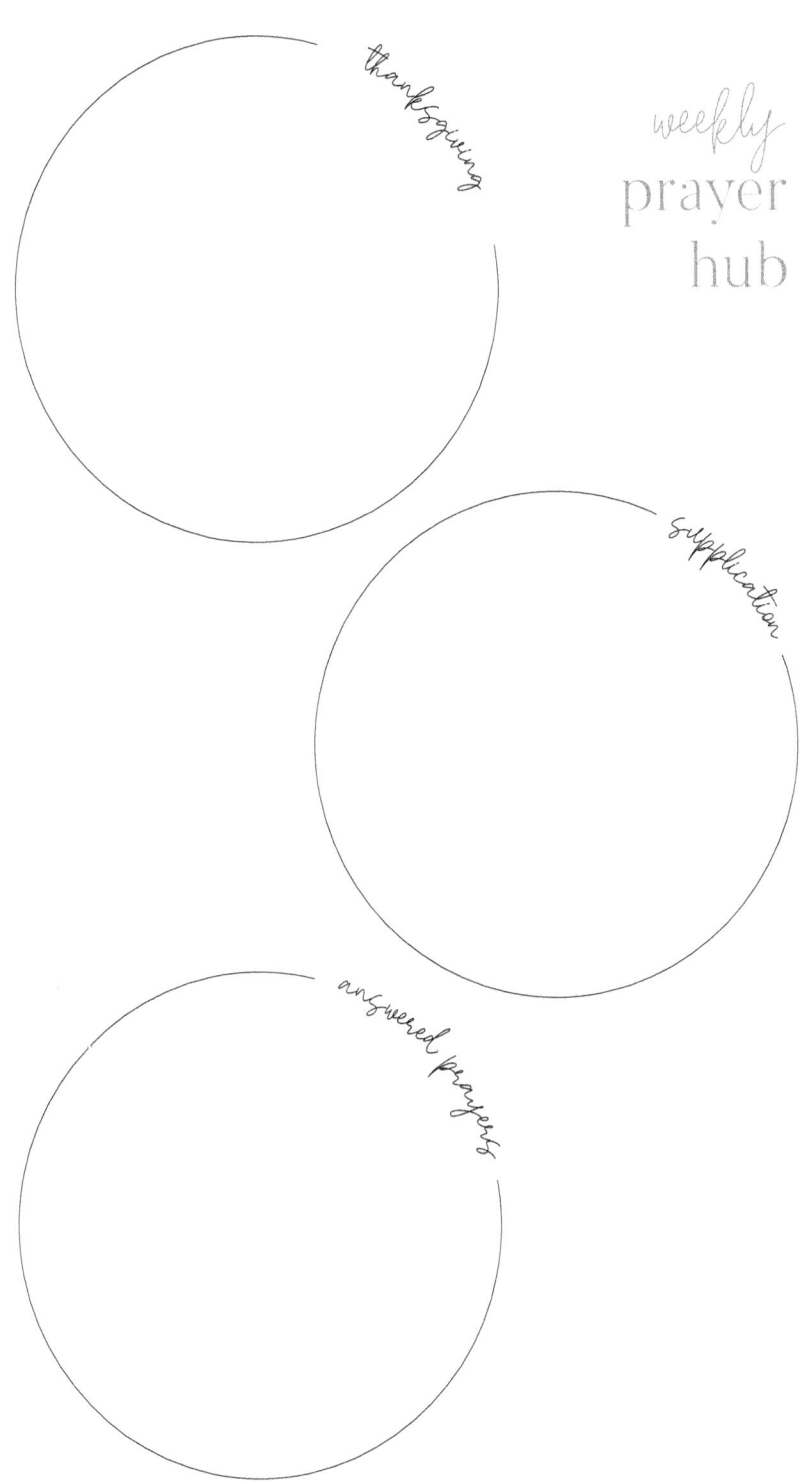

weekly prayer hub

thanksgiving

supplication

answered prayers

WEEK OF

weekly
prayer
hub

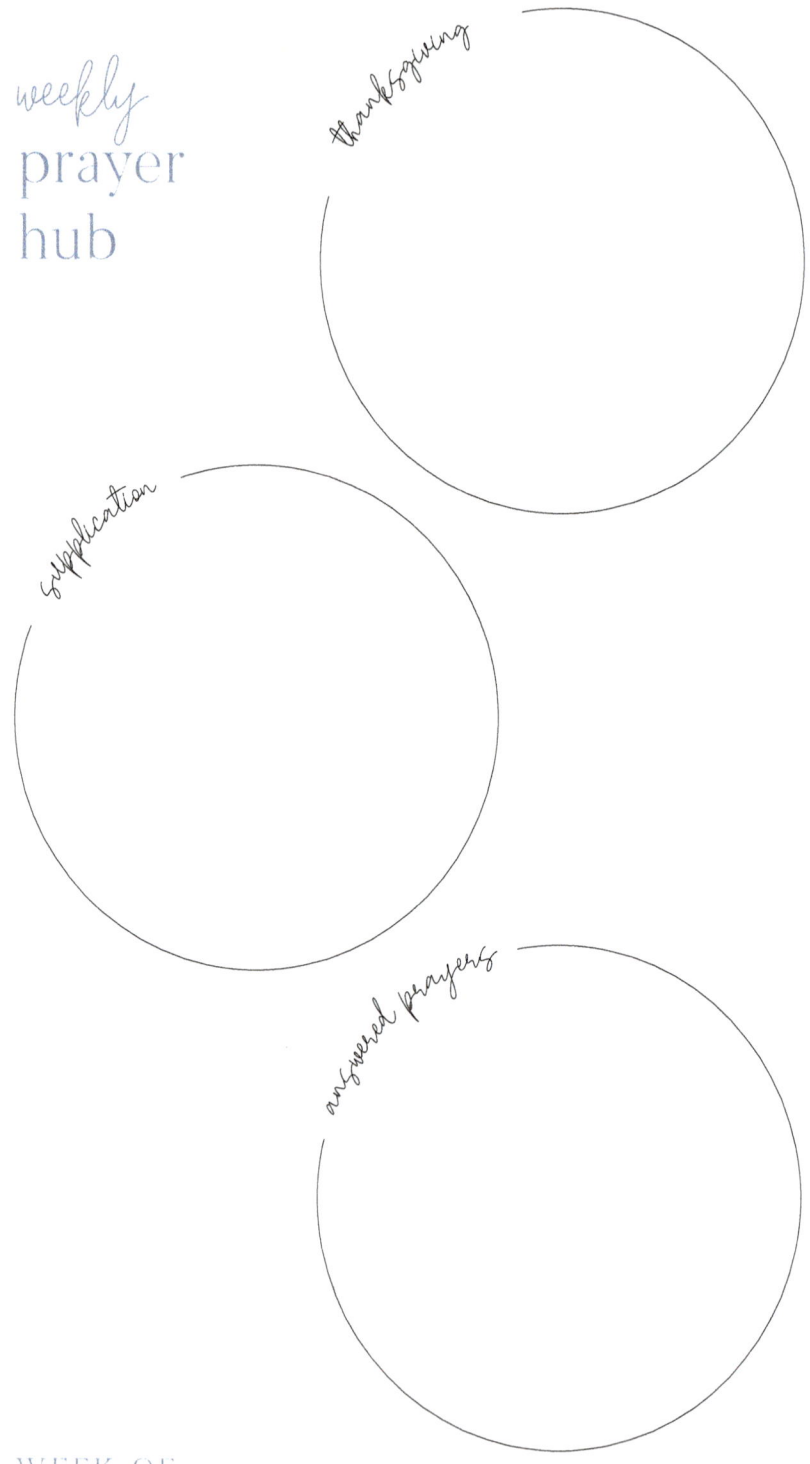

thanksgiving

supplication

answered prayers

WEEK OF

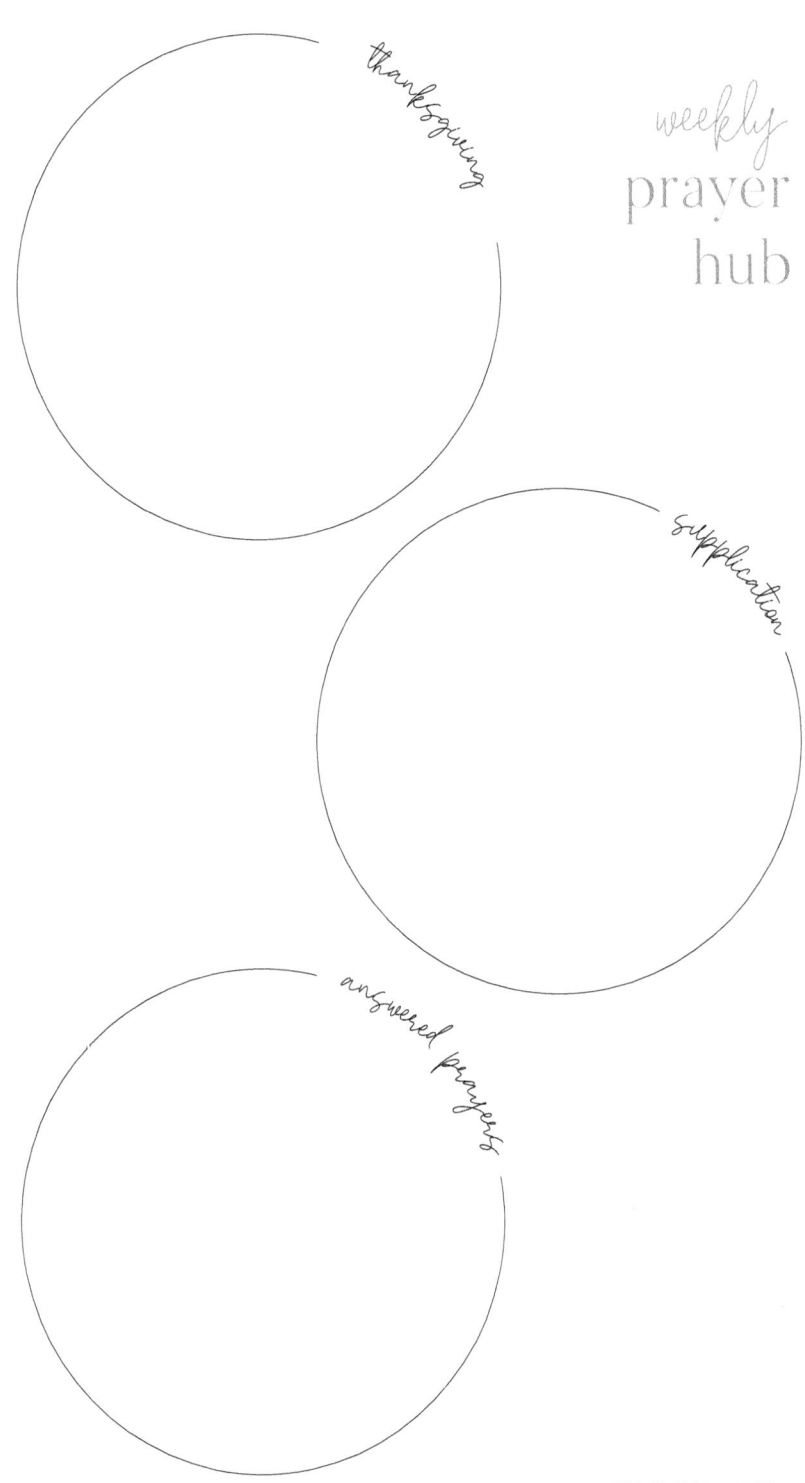

weekly
prayer
hub

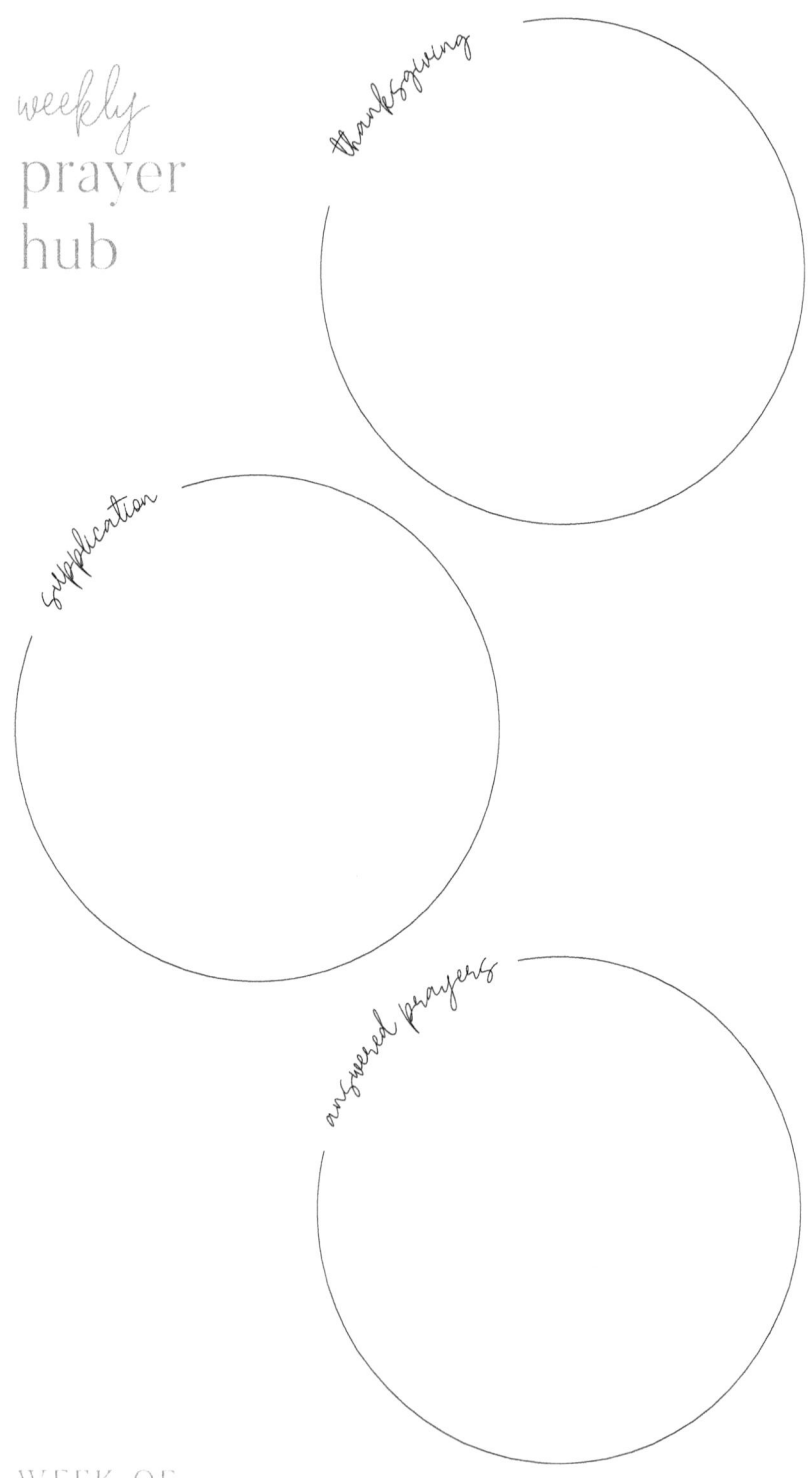

thanksgiving

supplication

answered prayers

WEEK OF

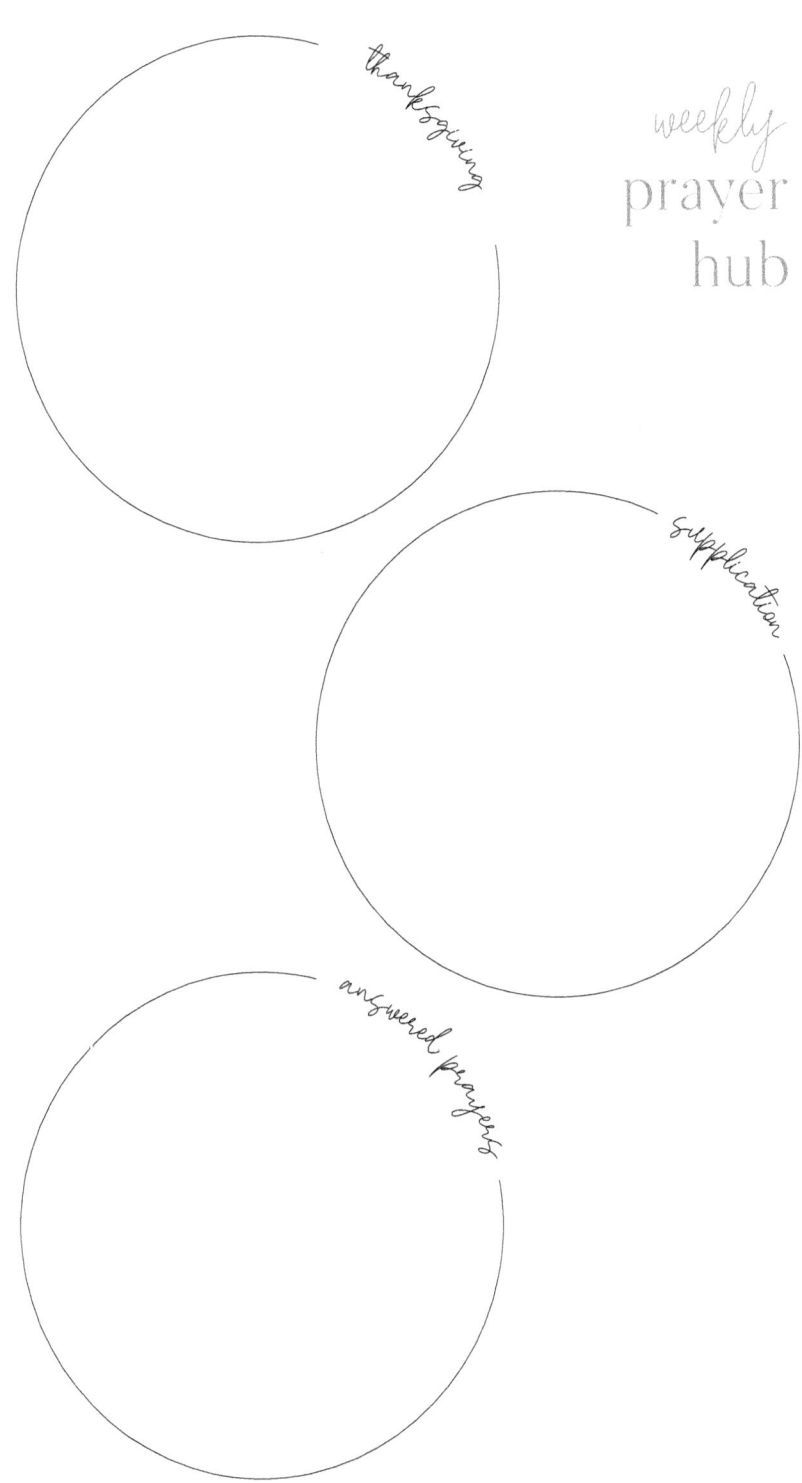

Behold, I will do a new thing, Now it shall spring forth; Shall you not know it? I will even make a road in the wilderness And rivers in the desert.

ISAIAH 43:19 NKJV

SECTION 4

rhēma

hray`-mah

Rhēma means "utterance" or "spoken word" in Greek. What is God speaking to you specifically in this present moment? Is it through prophecy, a dream or vision, or is it just a new revelation the Lord has given you through the reading of his word? Don't let it pass by, write it down or sketch it here.

DATE _____

"Every single person on this planet is worth the trouble we might face in the context of sharing Christ with them."

LISA HARPER

DATE _____

DATE _____

_____
_____
_____
_____
_____
_____
_____
_____
_____
_____
_____

_____	Fear not, for I am
_____	with you; Be not
_____	dismayed, for I
_____	am your God. I
_____	will strengthen
_____	you, Yes, I will
_____	help you, I will
_____	uphold you with
_____	My righteous
_____	right hand.'
_____	ISAIAH 41: NKJV

DATE _____

DATE _____

> Prayer is the portal that brings the power of heaven down to earth. It is kryptonite to the enemy and to all his ploys against you
>
> PRISCILLA SHIRER

DATE _____

DATE _____

> Cause me to hear Your lovingkindness in the morning, For in You do I trust; Cause me to know the way in which I should walk, For I lift up my soul to You.
>
> PSALM 143:8 NKJV

DATE

DATE _____

> I decided that if I could teach my daughter anything about herself, it would be that because a good God made the woman, then being a woman was a good thing.
>
> JACKIE HILL PERRY

DATE _____

DATE _____

> Wise women tuck Godly wisdom into the words they speak and even more into the words they choose not to speak.
>
> LYSA TERKEURST

DATE _____

DATE _____

> For I know the thoughts that I think toward you, says the Lord, thoughts of peace and not of evil, to give you a future and a hope.
>
> JEREMIAH 29:11 NKJV

DATE _____

DATE _____

> The mind feasts on what it focuses on. What consumes my thinking will be the making or the breaking of my identity.
>
> LYSA TERKEURST

DATE _____

DATE _____

> Trust in the Lord with all your heart, And lean not on your own understanding; In all your ways acknowledge Him, And He shall direct your paths.
>
> PROVERBS 3:5-6

DATE

DATE _____

> The decisions you're making today will impact your tomorrows.
>
> PRISCILLA SHIRER

DATE _____

DATE _____

> There's power in allowing yourself to be known and heard, in owning your unique story, in using your authentic voice.
>
> — MICHELLE OBAMA

DATE _____

DATE _____

And we know that all things work together for good to those who love God, to those who are the called according to His purpose.

ROMANS 8:28

DATE _____

DATE _____

> If you're always trying to be normal, you will never know how amazing you can be.
>
> MAYA ANGELOU

DATE _____

DATE _____

> These things I have spoken to you, that in Me you may have peace. In the world you will have tribulation; but be of good cheer, I have overcome the world.
>
> JOHN 16:33 NKJV

DATE _____

DATE _____

> Fight for the things that you care about, but do it in a way that will lead others to join you.
>
> RUTH BADER GINSBURG

DATE _____

DATE _____

> Let us hold fast the confession of our hope without wavering, for He who promised is faithful.
>
> HEBREWS 10:23 NKJV

DATE _____

DATE _____

> Jesus didn't come to make us safe. He came to make us dangerous to the kingdom of darkness.
>
> — CHRISTINE CAINE

DATE _____

DATE _____

> Finally, brethren, whatever things are true, whatever things are noble, whatever things are just, whatever things are pure, whatever things are lovely, whatever things are of good report, if there is any virtue and if there is anything praiseworthy—meditate on these things.
>
> PHILIPPIANS 4:8 NKJV

DATE _____

DATE _____

> Passion is the log that keeps the fire of purpose blazing.
>
> OPRAH WINFREY

DATE _____

DATE _____

> So he answered and said to me: "This is the word of the Lord to Zerubbabel: 'Not by might nor by power, but by My Spirit,' Says the Lord of hosts.
>
> ZECHARIAH 4:6 NKJV

DATE _____

DATE _____

> You've never gone too far that God can't redeem you, restore you, forgive you, and give you a second chance.
>
> LYSA TERKEURST

DATE _____

DATE _____

> If you are not royalty, He is not King.
>
> BETH MOORE

DATE

DATE _____

> But seek first the kingdom of God and His righteousness, and all these things shall be added to you.
>
> MATTHEW 6:33 NKJV

DATE _____

DATE _____

> As you give God your time, your gifts, your resources and talents, He will use them to have a critically important and eternal impact on this world.
>
> CHRISTINE CAINE

DATE _____

DATE _____

> Behold, I will do a new thing, Now it shall spring forth; Shall you not know it? I will even make a road in the wilderness And rivers in the desert.
>
> ISAIAH 43:19 NKJV

DATE _____

DATE _____

> A season when it's just you and Jesus can sometimes lead to the most important thing you were put on earth to do.
>
> BETH MOORE

DATE _____

DATE _____

> Nothing—nothing!—is too far gone that your God cannot resurrect it.
>
> PRISCILLA SHIRER

DATE _____

DATE _____

Your word is a lamp to my feet And a light to my path.

PSALM 119:105 NKJV

DATE _____

DATE _____

> Her success does not threaten mine.
> — LYSA TERKEURST

DATE _____

DATE _____

> Blessed is the man who trusts in the Lord, And whose hope is the Lord.
>
> JEREMIAH 17:7 NKJV

DATE _____

DATE _____

> When we feed our faith, we starve our doubts.
>
> CHRISTINE CAINE

DATE _____

DATE _____

> When God says go forward, don't even think about standing still.
>
> BETH MOORE

DATE _____

DATE _____

> God is the God of "right now." He doesn't want you sitting around regretting yesterday. Nor does He want you wringing your hands and worrying about the future. He wants you focusing on what He is saying to you and putting in front of you... right now
>
> PRISCILLA SHIRER

DATE _____

DATE _____

> And do not be conformed to this world, but be transformed by the renewing of your mind, that you may prove what is that good and acceptable and perfect will of God.
>
> ROMANS 12:2 NKJV

DATE _____

DATE _____

> I love this truth-filled reminder that the victory is already ours, the battle is already won; we have more than conquered whatever this world will try to throw at us because we're God's children.
>
> CHRISTINE CAINE

DATE _____

DATE _____

> I can do all things through Christ who strengthens me.
> PHILIPPIANS 4:13 NKJV

DATE _____

DATE _____

> God's real desire, in addition to displaying His glory, is to claim your heart and the hearts of those you love.
>
> PRISCILLA SHIRER

DATE _____

DATE _____

> It's impossible to hold up the banners of victim and victory at the same time.
>
> — LYSA TERKEURST

DATE _____

DATE _____

> Blessed is the man who endures temptation; for when he has been approved, he will receive the crown of life which the Lord has promised to those who love Him.
>
> JAMES 1:12 NKJV

DATE _____

DATE _____

> The Lord takes pleasure in those who fear Him, In those who hope in His mercy.
>
> PSALMS 147:11 NKJV

DATE _____

DATE _____

> Do you not know that you are the temple of God and that the Spirit of God dwells in you?
>
> I CORINTHIANS 3:16 NKJV

DATE _____

DATE _____

For with God nothing will be impossible.

LUKE 1:37 NKJV

DATE _____

DATE _____

> Whenever I am afraid, I will trust in You.
>
> PSALMS 56:3 NKJV

DATE _____

Go therefore and make disciples of all the nations, baptizing them in the name of the Father and of the Son and of the Holy Spirit, teaching them to observe all things that I have commanded you; and lo, *I am with you always, even to the end of the age. Amen.*

MATTHEW 28:19-20

SECTION 5

conclusion

PROMPTS

Has the vision of your calling changed since starting this journal? If so, write out the new vision God has given you. If not, what clarity has He given you about your calling?

_____
_____
_____
_____
_____
_____

Have your goals changed or shifted? How has God prepared or equipped you to reach these goals?

_____
_____
_____
_____
_____
_____
_____

How has God moved in your life in the past few months? Has He answered prayers, opened doors or moved in certain situations on your behalf? Reflect on that here.

_____
_____
_____
_____
_____
_____
_____
_____
_____
_____
_____
_____
_____
_____
_____
_____
_____
_____
_____
_____
_____
_____
_____
_____

www.ingramcontent.com/pod-product-compliance
Lightning Source LLC
Chambersburg PA
CBHW041323110526
44592CB00021B/2804